Ghost Hunt

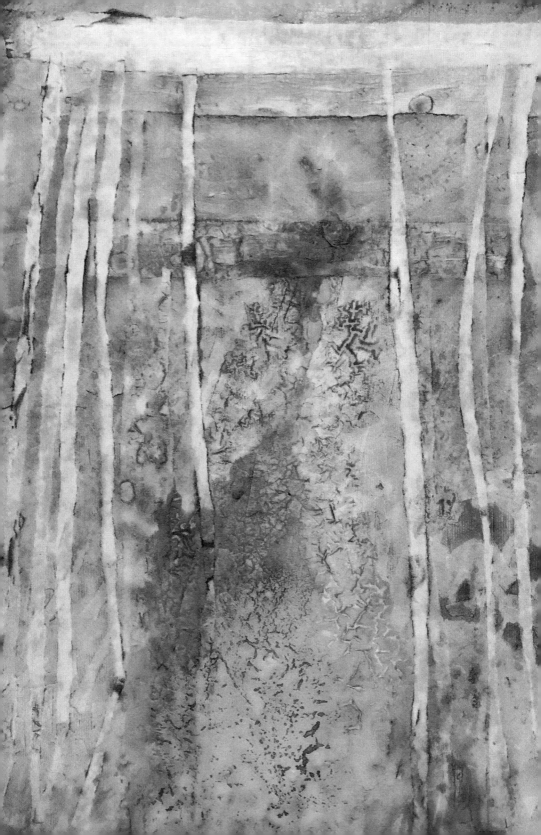

Ghost Hunt
Mac Gay

POETRY

THE **BLACK SPRING**
PRESS GROUP

First published in 2023
by The Black Spring Press Group
An Eyewear Publishing imprint
Maida Vale, London W9,
United Kingdom

Typeset with graphic design by Edwin Smet
Cover painting by Edwin Smet

The right of Mac Gay to be identified as author of
this work has been asserted in accordance with section 77
of the Copyright, Designs and Patents Act 1988

ISBN 978-1-913606-78-7

Editor's note: the author has requested that American spelling and grammar be used in this work.

BLACKSPRINGPRESSGROUP.COM

Mac Gay is the author of several collections of poetry, including *Farm Alarm*, runner up for Texas Review Press 2018 Robert Phillips Poetry Chapbook Prize, and, more recently, *Our Fatherlessness*, from The Orchard Street Press, Ltd. His poems have appeared in many journals, including *Atlanta Review, Crosswinds, Cutbank, E-Verse Radio, Ironwood, Plainsong*, and *The American Journal of Poetry*. He teaches at Perimeter College of Georgia State University and lives with his wife Jana, 2 dogs and 4 cats in Covington, Georgia.

Table of Contents

Back Then

The past is never dead. It's not even past.

William Faulkner

AN E. B. WHITE READER

From the sunny back pew, we boys saw
the shadow of my head's unruly hair
proceed across the preacher's face, and knew
we'd seen the light, praise all three stooges.
I'd lean my head a certain way, and shade
would follow, instant as a bad choice.
Devilishness was the spirit that moved,
quicker, even, than a smartass Baptist boy.
Oh, I was bright, but also I was dark —
a student, even then, of the twists and turns
of country duende. And I was widely read,
I thought, so I tore a quick stencil out
of the bulletin and let the light project
some sly and worldly wisdom on the wall
behind the choir beside the preacher's head.
Some Pig, it said, but no one later shined
enough to appreciate my allusion. Instead
they took the quote for Charlie Manson, saw
my light's effusion as helter skelter painted
on the icebox of the Lord. The choir's gossip
stole my comic riches. My father stormed
out back to cut some switches.

LITTLE LEAGUE LESSON

Developed my flair for hyperbole
back when Clayton our shortstop
sliced his arm wide open on the unsafety-
glassed dagger left in Mrs. Swann's window
that our stray baseball had smashed.
His blood left a trail like a loud disturbing
wail that hangs in the mind
and raises *your* blood drip drip
all shiny and red down the sidewalk
and on up the stairs drip drip.
How could a body contain so much blood?
I said to myself as I followed the trail.
Such exsanguination made me
queasy and pale and certain
ol' Clayton was dead, yet

there he was next day, gigantic
bandage over 32 stitches, but cocky
as ever and crammed full of color,
tan as a Georgia peach,
while I remained pale.

Me: How can he be ok
minus all that blood?

Dad: With shit or piss or blood,
a little is a flood.
Stay out of the dark side of your head
where the bad thoughts multiply.
Sleep at night and think in the light.
For with blood, as with its abstractions:
suffering and death,
(said soon-to-die Dad)
a little goes a long way.

CLOSURE

That's what Dad always wanted.
"Close the door behind you," he'd snap,
or "Did you take out the trash?" The man
hated loose ends, any task dragging
from one day into the next. "You
finish your algebra?" he'd fling at me
blind from behind his newspaper.
Or "Let's finish trimming these hedges
before darkness takes us over."
(Nothing was worse than uneven
Red-tip Photinias.) But the thing
he hated most was getting old:
"Old men are like broken tools
or leaky buckets," he said,
"or the invisible man in the movies,
just fading and fading until he'd
have to wrap himself with rolls of gauze
just so folks would know he was still there."
So Mom took some comfort later
from his bad good luck. That
Sunday morning he left with Bo
to put a neck yoke on the crazy cow
that kept jumping over the fence.
He aimed to be through before church,
and he was, almost: unconscious
as a stone by noon, but
his dawdling heart kept
beating till half past five.

THE PHOTO

Fourteen, and fresh off the bus from school,
I had a snack and then was very bored.
I saw where Mom had had the family Bible
out, discovered tucked in Song of Songs
an ancient black-and-white of a dazzling girl.
The printing on the back in Dad's neat block
draftsman hand said "Mary Gay Pitts, 22, new
bride of Dr. J. W. Pitts, in her red Ford coupe,
a wedding gift from her husband." Wait, no way
this was my grouchy great aunt Mamie, still
living by herself just up the road. She then was
eighty-eight, stick-skinny, green persimmon-bitter.
Yet *this* devilishly pretty woman warmed me
hotter than a campfire stone. Peeping out beneath
her long dark skirt – a feast of fine bare leg, neat
ankles, perfect feet. How could time have wreaked
such havoc on one so young and fair? I'd think about
that later, when I had the time. Only an hour remained
before they'd all pour home from work: Just barely
time to steal this Mary to my room, then before
they all crashed in, get her back in the good book.

THE LAST WORD

Fifteen and a half and full of it, I was,
and Susan Cooper had asked me to a dance.

Only six months till I get the real thing, Dad.
I have my learner's permit on my hip,
and I can drive as good as you, I said.
Why can't I have the car on Friday night,
instead of you driving us like babies?

Because you are a young ungrateful fool,
I'd tell myself if now could speak to then.

But spoiled and full of piss, I picked a fight
with him on his way to the kitchen
for a glass of milk to calm his ulcer: me.
I wound my anger tight as it would twist
and let it fly full force into that room.
I still can feel our last long hard glare,
and then he turned, all done, back down the hall.
But then, goddamn it, I just couldn't quit;
I hurled *I hate you!* mean as I could yell.
Yet on he walked to bed, then to his
fatal misstep with that crazy cow at dawn.

But fifty years of silence can yell, too.

DAD'S PRIOR COMMITMENT

After Dad was killed, no one came
but the cows when I called.
Old Man Hill let me work on his farm,
but he already had a dear son.
Rattling around the spare world
like a BB in a beer can,
I could stretch in my emptiness
like a liquid filling a crack,
or a rattler that waits in a sack.
I adopted a passive role, waiting
and waiting, like fishing, yet
in all my youth, no bite. Alone
in your head, there's no one to fight
but yourself, till the cows come home.

OUR FATHERLESSNESS

No fence around my foolishness,
I've zigged and zagged from sane
to daft and back again.
I'd steal, bestow, assuage,
then, snap, like lightning, rage.
Dad, back when I was small,
the big Holstein that smashed
your head into that rough barn
wall, she crushed into the nasty
floor my best chance to survive.

Since then I've bounced off all
four walls of night. It's tough
without a dad to point what's right.
Alone, I've fished and fumbled,
flung my head into the jumble,
but the fog has rarely cleared.
I've wasted, wounded, sabotaged
my angel with dumb mumbling.
In Pyrrhic angry back-and-forths
I've laid waste with my tongue.
Seems I just can't win for losing.
Fucking up is not amusing.

In tangled pathless laurel hells,
how many boys lie rotting in the weeds?
The universe seems empty as our
house after you died. Fatherless
means wild, hellacious, lost. Free
tickets to condemned amusement parks.
Rides at these unfair fairs are dangerous.
I fly lone through the dark and dream of us.

BACK THEN

Back then the strength of the South
was in the hay and the trees,
in the blank spaces to fill up,
in the simple fact that the whole thing
had not come to fruition.
The sky then was blue with hope
and not just blue.
The air then was clear as a good idea,
and the streams drooled sweet
as your own child.

Now we don't know what to say.
Now we've said too much.
But back then there was such silence
that your great-great
grandfather could say something
stupid and everyone laughed and agreed
with his quaint old white shrieking
beard just because it could speak.
Then the creeks were so pure
and the trees so big
that not even the dark star
of a man hanging there
could change the flag.

MAGICIAN

Back in 1980, when Billy Roberts'
crazy teenage brother Norris
tried to make a Rabbit disappear,
we all filed into the back lot
at the Ford place to see
just how close he'd come.
Pretty close, we found out:
To his credit, Norris and a good
portion of the mangled
Volkswagen were gone.

PRACTICE

"It keeps 'em out of trouble."
– Coach Wilbur Fisher

I hated football practice. But it
was a necessary blender: In it
we threw the hormonal demons
of ourselves to be chopped
and spun until all the potentially
lethal juices, the poisons
and the acids, could be mixed
with the healthy air over the green
grass of the fairground in closed
sessions behind chain link.
Bull in the Ring, Oklahoma Drills,
the pitting of one raw soul
against another – best not seen,
like the making of sausage. Yet
those violent discombobulations
were nostalgically worshiped
by our over-the-hill fathers.

Only our mothers could see
the wars raging in our selves,
the blood we drank to survive,
and were frightened by the nerve
of their little supernovas
who could have robbed banks,
slaughtered friends and neighbors,
who could have burned entire
villages, raping the women
and eating the dogs, were it not
for the coaches, with their deep
knowledge of young fire, who
paced daily under the tortuous sun,
hell-bent to tame the damn lions.

SCORN

for Susan

Grudge-fuck is a funny word
that at sixteen I'd never heard,
so what you did, it had no name,
but you did it just the same.
My best friend Bill had let you go
for a hotter Susan, blond as snow.
In turn, you set your sights on me,
after the dance, since I was free.
I didn't know a place to park;
You said that Bill's dad's store was dark.
Furniture was what he sold;
New mattresses were manifold.
You knew where his dad hid the key,
exclaimed *I really have to pee!*
You slipped in, peed, then mimed said word,
then on Bill's desk you shat a turd.

SQUIRREL CREEK FARM

The pecans and the oaks twitched round the place:
Scads of squirrels zoomed through arboreal space.
The acorns and the pecans fed them well,
but fear of fire sent myriad squirrels to hell.
Chewed wires in the attic sealed their fate —
both brothers honed their fear into a hate
that necessitated gunplay in their heads.
They filled up umpteen buckets with the dead
and dumped those once-quick critters in the creek.
(Perhaps the sin's not eating hunted meat.)
That creek was worried red by gunfire's mess,
but what flowed down came back around, I guess:
Just next year, incessant spring rains flooded.
Squirrel Creek swelled, unleashed its repressed id
and swept that hot-wired house clean off its piers.
(I see it float and burn across the years.)
Their mother trapped inside was never found.
Somehow a crazy narrative got round —
some storied, country foolishness, enhanced —
that on its flaming gable, gray squirrels danced.
Both brothers ended in the Asian war.
I guess blood sticks its foot inside death's door.

FRANK STANFORD

1948-1978

Though I never met him, we arrived
same summer, same year, both our daddies
old engineers, both of us privileged
white boys spoiled by our mamas
into a kind of Fauntleroyesque corner
escaped only by stark hyperbole —
blood, say, or death.
Unbeknownst to us, we had entered
this world where our inappropriate remarks
become appropriate. Yet such stews
make for odd tastes, confused
dichotomies: a succotash of black and white,
up and down, pink and blue,
life and death. Almost
a junction of conjunctions.
But Frank was an altogether different
kettle of fight, of write, of do —
and so he did, writing best words in best
order, so frictionless they shot all
the way into the twenty-first century.
Yet he overlooked a major importance:
himself, stuck back there in the ditch
of the seventies,
one ditch beyond Elvis,
stranded eternal beside the way through.

AGAINST ROMANTICISM

for Frank Stanford

Don't let this life get in the way
of your death, said Frank
through his handsome teeth,
composing himself. His three
bullets put their money where
his mouth was, his myth is. After
such redundant punctuation,
his stunned silence
soaked out in all directions.

Drama aside, it's a major loss
to our profit: We'd only
the requisite three score and ten
to glean his best-said zen, at best,
so why rush the worms with
that rash ratatat of lead?
Death's lead has gravitas, sure,
but the gold of life is denser,
weightier with its wealth,
so why not pan for it?

If he'd made that last hard hill,
I'd like to think he'd arrived
at a better other side, the downhill ride
to a level land in which to leave
his black cape behind. I'd like to think
he'd have chosen not to choose
that permanent solution to
a temporary problem, no longer
trusting anyone under thirty's
thousand feet per second hyperbole.

RE: THE LOST FARM

That ground once sweetly tenanted...
– Robert Penn Warren

Dear Dad,
The farm's changed hands *again*.
From Shoal Creek Road I saw
they've torn the lot fence down.
Cows graze the seeded row crop land,
yet both of Granddad's barns still stand.
Big colorful machines are everywhere.

Pardon me for selling it. Most
foolish thing I ever did: investing
in the Brooklyn Bridge of poetry.
My poems, these crippled things,
don't often fly, yet they're airmail,
of sorts, addressed to you. I hear
their grating whine, and maybe
if that pen of pigs we raised back
then could fly, then so could you.

I write each morning as the others sleep.
Like I was sleeping when you rose
that dawn and left to fix the fence
and yoke the crazy cow that tore it down.
She tore you down forever hence.
Now half a century's silence since,
time's mythologized every single simple
thing. It's made you rise up like a moon
that stares its faint incessant glow.
It makes the farm a promised land,
and when I ask to enter, it says no.

Love Songs

Nothing is ever entirely right in the lives of those who love each other.

Eavan Boland

HOME

We began somewhere near here,
a haystack behind us, the sky
seemed a good idea
at the time. Problems
were hidden out there, plenty good,
for the kitchen was a place
the whole world came down to
to drink. Even the dead
shined white and painless
from their clean stones.
And the hay was behind us,
domes of green promise,
each hiding a white house,
a mother and father.
Each its own meadow,
its own mule,
its own picnic for winter,
which is now.

HOW ANNIVERSARIES START

That double seat back at the Strand
mandated Jane's vigilant tracking of hands.
Then only lips kept them joined at the hip
in their house-a-fire freshmen exuberance.
Both had hurried like hell to be
late-50s cool and late-50s swell
till going steady's glue increasingly bound
them tighter than Edgar and Annabelle Lee.
Both barely teenage yet stretching themselves
toward taller, smarter, all-grown-up ardor.
And all each week long for almost a year
Dean inscribed notebooks, desks, trees,
with hearts circling D.G.+ J.E.
Way back then Dean loved her non-stop,
his hormonal groans growing grown.
Such sweet young love, completely their own,
yet real-world postponement thinned to when,
not if, for young Dean's raw passion,
though green, was quite stiff. Soon
premature nuptials from jumping the gun
in the blink of an eye shocked both kids with a son.

ODE TO MEAT

Meat is muscle, right? Like Schwarzenegger's
pec. We carnivores say what the heck,
we're going to eat the part that moves your feet
when you run fast, or maybe savory tissue
that helps you wag your tail. It smells good
on the grill, so good it makes my mind
forget the way you looked with fur, or
back when feathers sailed you through the air.
After we killed you dead, dry lice-filled
feathers just got in the way. Anyway,

flight's over when your purpose shifts
from you to me. You sizzle in a way that makes
me free of how you shone up in the tree
like God's bright thoughts of red or brown or blue;
or ran fast, big and brown, across the ground.
The good Lord lets me catch you with this hound.
The power of your incense from this pan
reiterates meat's good and right and true.
I sit and bow my head and say my grace.
I'm grateful I'm the swine that's eating you.

'60S LOVE

We boys had myriad hands,
for the hands, not the penis,
were the measure of a man.
In the game of Drive-in,
the goal line was never crossed
(at least no time soon), yet
the hands were expected to be
always searching for that sweet
valentine hidden in her clothes,
though mostly all it really was
was holding hands, for she
would deftly counter your
movements, swiftly grab your
hand and gently move it
back to the starting position.
So you'd settle again into
the lull of kissing, then
subtly, smoothly as possible,
begin to strive again for those
precious treats there in her blouse
or the bonanza at the top of
her smooth bare leg. At the Moonlit,
the disappointment of the evening
might be pantyhose, or, worse,
a girdle, that not-so-subtle finality.
The girdle was dating armor,
the chastity belt of 1965, and
when you encountered its steel
smoothness at the top of a soft thigh
your heart would slow and you'd
hear inside of that tongueless kiss
the sound of your own sigh.

KISSING THE DEAD GIRL

40 years back we met at camp –
Camp Wahsega, a Cherokee word
that means charming 8th. grade girlfriend,
or lovely early-maturing female,
or love in the North Georgia woods,
or kissing pretty girl in the rain,
or one day you'll both be forgotten
as dust. Yet we knew that last
translation was far far away.

And 40 years later, warming up
for a race, I found myself running
the graveyard back home, but
the warming up cooled really quick
when I saw Bonnie's grave.
Can a man race when his mind
remains at such a surprising place?
I'll tell you, only the mind races.
For kissing dead girls is a punch
in the gut. Now the dust soon mine
is her forever home. So each year
I go back, place a kiss on her stone.

DEARESTS

It's always been two of us,
one of us changing herself like clothes.
The portrait on my desk
has a hundred channels.
At breakfast the egg
is the only stable face,
but you are like my poems:
all one poem,
and when I wash my face,
I'm washing all the windows
of the small motel
where we were married
like the faces of a crowd,
my little one.

ROADKILL APOCALYPSE

With collective growl, in unison they rise
from all corners of the blacktop-striped earth.
An eerie moan at first then builds to roar
till ear wax melts and human blood runs cold.
These furry, fanged, scaly, feathered Lazaruses
are back from dust, once smeared across roads,
diffuse, now pure reconstituted rage, a whole
century of poor critters, this karmic army of carrion,
perfect again on the some-odd dog-yeared
anniversary of the damnable contraption's first atrocity.
The undead dogs and cats join hordes of deer,
raccoon, opossum, skunk, coyote, snakes –
all shattered puzzles surrealistically solved
and raised to seething wholes to finally foil
the murderous machines and their geniuses
who laughed then swerved to score a cat;
or let the dog run loose next to the road.
O those that could not speak have had enough.
And all that spilled blood powers rage
like the devil's gasoline. God (spelled Dog
from right to left) seems fully on their side.
The myriad doomsday pack crushes cars, trucks,
and leaves no human hearts of stone unturned.
With awful gnashing teeth and razor claws,
they shred the metal back into the earth.
Their roar drowns out all human squawk and whine
and pushes devils back into their hells.
The righteous once-crushed underdogs have won.
And in my dream, fed-up, I grow
my arms to legs and join their cause.

DREAM'S ANARCHY

Nostalgia almost makes old chaos sweet
because it's tucked back safely in the past.
The worst that almost was is made effete
forever by good luck that came to pass.

So when I say you almost drowned that night,
(just a quaint adventure, now we're old)
the *almost* makes that dread seem nearly light
which way back then was helpless, stark, and cold.

Still, nightmares of that time do often come
and stir my peaceful sleep to stark unrest.
In dreams I know you're deep below the hum
of rescue vessels searching east, west,

north and south, dragging that dark chill lake.
Then, thankfully, your cold feet help me wake.

SUBLIMATION

Straight to vapor, snow will often go.
It skips the shapeless liquid part
and zips straight to its heaven in the air.
Impatient, that is where you went,
my stillborn star. This foolish
treading water in this life
must have seemed too slow,
the shore too far, water too deep
for you to hang around for years and watch
substantial things you learned to love
turn dust and make you weep.
Still, I wish that you'd dropped by
and visited your mom and me.
For though all passes, there is much to see.

NOW THE OLD LOVES

Now the old loves seem like
liquor the doctor has forbidden,
or the recollection of thunderstorms
sweetly recalled in the dry season,
with memory's surprise gift of
the perfect scent of petrichor.
What I'd give for those storms,
even the ones that tore things down
in their instant violence of painful
subtraction. Then was such happy
derangement of lips and skin
that eventually exited like a death.
Such sharp remembrance, even now,
years from the torrential bliss,
seems more real than the present.
A different kind of longing now,
those young years recalled from
way out here in the numbness of age.
Even the tremors of explosions
from the adjacent quarry seem tame.
Just trying to remain now
is the one dry adventure.
This species of loneliness
is a burdensome coldness,
weightless snow sifting silently
like the imperceptible settling
of dirt on a mounded grave.

MY TRUCK

This truck has lasted long like I'd like to.
Its paint is dull, its fender has been smashed.
The old transmission slips out of 3rd. gear,
yet without thinking now I boogaloo
it back in gear before momentum's trashed —
all smooth as glass. Oh yeah, there was the rear
end crash, minor, that left the bumper bent,
just one more scar that might deface a car,
but added character to this pink truck.
One cool thing is that my truck's extant
yet unique from all others near or far,
in part because of accidental luck,
or lack thereof. The best: It still runs fine.
Its miles and scars and dents still roll through time.

News Flash

But what it is all about exactly I could no more say, at the present moment, than take up my bed and walk.

Samuel Beckett

PLUTO'S DESPAIR

It must have felt somewhat
like having another manuscript
rejected; or being taken out
of the starting lineup; or
the trauma of learning
the dark spot on your lung
is of dour and grave concern.
Heck, here you've been
A-list for years, part and
parcel of the pantheon,
"one of the nine best ever,"
according to the old *Almanac
of Science*, and though
nowhere near the largest,
certainly the most distant,
the most cryptic and aloof,
secluded in the hinterlands,
enigmatic as Salinger.

So was it chance that did
you in, or bad astrology,
or simply just your own
faux-pas: something you did
or did not do? Maybe
better attendance at those
tedious planetary meetings;
maybe some condescending
coolness toward the others.
But it wasn't your colleagues
that booted you out, no —
it was the scientists, those
specks with their galactic minds:
meddlers who measure us all.

THE ART OF SURPRISE

Some poets are better than others.
The best change directions in almost
every line, slapping your face,
or jerking your tie, like the Tilt-A-Whirl
at our fair each fall, or the small
jittery roller coaster that not many

may know Emily Dickinson invented,
at least on paper, with her plunges
and twists, surprises that even today
leave you walking from the page
in a crooked straight line. It's a ride
James Tate bought the rights to in the next
century, and right there in Amherst!

But when it comes to leaping poetry,
my seventh-grade squeeze, Doris
Witherspoon, surpassed even Robert Bly:
After two hot dogs, cotton candy,
a candy apple, the roller coaster, then
that Tilt-A-Whirl, the stuff she threw
up in my lap was the strongest last line.

NEWS FLASH

Two dead in murder/suicide,
it said. Two more I did not
know, and never will. Unless
some heaven waits far out
there still. Yet there's no word
from those I've known.
What's gone is gone, from
all I've seen or heard. The
graveyard is the most inert
place on earth. Even
the breeze there makes
no haste. So I can't help but
wonder why one of said two
would try so hard to race
beyond this tasty pie
of animation. The hearse
the husband chose has no
reverse, and postal service
sucks from that null nation.

ALARM SYSTEM

Raising her arrow ears, our
couched Chihuahua's chemicals
concoct into dynamite
awaiting detonation.
The mailman lights her fuse,
her cacophony conscripting
our catatonic other cur
who concurs in an instant,
the dead-to-the-world raised
like a loud-mouthed Lazarus
lashing out at a Bethany
that wrote him off as done.
*Push the envelope and pull
back a nub*, they bark, these
roiling, little-but-loud dust
devils beneath the doorknob,
wee allies of the rain, heat, and snow.

GOLD, EVEN WITHOUT ACCEPTANCE AND FAME

Losing another pen to the La-Z-Boy
brings me to the end of my rope, then
to my knees behind my throne of inspiration,
my temple of the Muse, my clinic
of do-it-yourself proctology.
In recovery mode, I unzip
the chair back's Velcro strip and
five pens tumble out, three bottle caps,
a handkerchief, and seventy-four
cents in change. My beautiful red
bone-handled pocket knife that
my daughter gave me last Christmas
slides out as well, along with an
embarrassing volume of crumbs.
It's like a fruitful metal detecting
expedition, or unearthing the ole
fifth grade time capsule.

And when the Velcro zips, I feel great
release, like when popping the pusy
pimple of my abscessed past with
a sharp and well-placed poem.
It's a treasure hunt, pussy-footing
around on the Ouija board of the page.
Even if the screeners don't like it,
and the judges never see it, I like
drilling these exploratory holes
in my grave way before I lie down.
There's gold for me down there, worth
more, even, than seventy-four cents.

It's better than golf or fishing, although
it's a kind of both. It keeps my brain
from twiddling its thumbs, or sucking them,
while our Seth Thomas ticks away on the mantle,
and more dog hairs accrue on the couch.

THE BOY

At the interview with Bob in personnel,
the boy said, "But I have no experience."
"Nonsense," said Bob, "You're an old hand
at being a boy." Bob installed the boy as head
of the Boys' Studies Program, and in the fall,
three new courses, *Pigtail Pulling as Rudimentary
Flirting, Stone Skimming 101*, and *Cane Pole
Fishing in Small Ponds,* appeared on the schedule.
We all knew Bob could place 'em with the best,
but this match was uncanny. The boy was good
and loved his work. Each day when we arrived
on campus, he'd already be white-washing the fence
beside the Academic Building. And we knew he
liked us because occasionally we'd find a dead cat
stinking in our cars. We'd see him barefoot, swinging
a mess of fish, climbing trees behind the parking lot,
or, in the evenings sometimes, he'd catch
toad frogs under the streetlight. He fit right in,
and we could always count on him for a laugh:
whoopee cushions, thumbtacks in chairs, goldfish
in the water cooler. He was with us for years,
changed the very culture: straw hats became
de rigueur. Yet somehow things went south: At 21,
for some odd reason, they gave him socks, shoes, a tie,
and the transfer – a demotion to the Division of Man.

RODEOISTIC

The only things that interest me
are the aberrations, like the ponderous
Holstein cows at the Mansfield Rodeo
hauled into service due to the bull shortage,
bucking straps puckering the hide
behind their massive mama udders,
their burgeoning bags sloshing absurdly
side to side under Rockette kicks.
The Wild West's weirdness is queer
as a ten-gallon hat's jonesing
to fly under the wind's radar,
yet the wind's wild hair leaves
the cowboy's bald bookkeeper pate
bare as a baby's butt
in confusion's dusty arena.

FUNDAMENTALIST

He's rock but also a wheel:
Tractor tire rolling uphill.
And that hill is Jesus's Calvary
with his goofy cross I call overkill,
but that's who he is. His eyes
can only read Bible. I'm liable
to call the man fool, but what
do I know? Believer or non, nobody
knows what's around death's corner.
At least I will say the man
sticks to his guns, that son of a gun.
He's clung to his roots and they've held
him down firm to this old red clay
ground where we both popped out
in the world. Now I've left, gone to sea,
and float on my ocean of doubt.
Yet seasickness tires a man some.
At least where he plows, dirt's solid.
I'm adrift in this indifferent, bottomless sea.
All that's left of my Sunday school ark
is oil slick, jetsam, flotsam.

PREVENTION'S OUNCE

Excessive prophylaxis is a curse.
The rubber chases tail to pregnancy.
And mostly warnings only warn
of self-fulfilling prophesy.
The watched ditch is magnet
for your terrified front tire, and
the HurryCane often predicts a fall.
Hypochondria prognosticates the hearse,
sometimes, as too much worry
rarely fails to throw prevention in reverse.
A dearth of peaceful sleep at night
guarantees a bad next day.
To overthink only inserts
confusion and delay.
Worry just hoists the bucket
with black water from the well.
It aids, not keeps away,
all those viruses from hell.
Failing to give a shit makes
all your troubles quit, I've often
heard the devil-may-care say,
but I don't know. My ulcer claims
some fretting helps the trouble cease,
or slow, at least. Being too blasé,
I'm pretty sure, assists bad luck,
provides it yeast. At best, worry
will pump beaucoup adrenaline
to fight when hell lets loose the beast.

MURMURATION

Before the 4 eyes of this man and dog
an oak sucked in a slew of starlings
from all points of the sky's outstretching,
then before the camera was out of the pocket
shook and slung sailing bright pieces
of dark shining in all directions.

Both man and dog stood transfixed
in astounded mammalian unknowing
by connection's whirring dovetailing.
Both were born in kindred convergence,
will pass in centrifugal scatter
into instant bereaving divergence.
Such purposeless yoyoing of being;
some arriving while others leaving.

WABI-SABI

So if you're a kid who's sour with the D
you dutifully earned in my 1101,
I extend an invitation to key my truck
out there rusting in the faculty lot —
I'm all for catharsis. Let off a little steam,
I always say. It's not like the banged-up
little clunker with a quarter million miles
or I will mind. Yet seventeen years back,
driving her home from the Toyota place,
I felt unease. This scratch magnet then
had flawless complexion. There is
such a thing as too much perfection.
I missed the comfy wreck I'd traded in.

But now, after all these ruts and miles,
three fender benders, dents, rust,
scratches, spilled paint in the bed,
ten sets of tires, a clutch, a busted head,
I love this heap that oddly looks like me.
I savor shifting her slipping, grinding gears,
smelling oil every time I turn the heater on,
riding in dust, dog hair, the rancid smell of sweat,
and the sweet fact that she's all paid off.

And as we ride satisfied toward the junkyard
at forty in a sixty mile per hour zone,
the best is seeing in the rearview all
the young, impatient hotshots fume and foam.

WITNESSING WEATHER

When they come they come
like a break in the fog.
Everything clears for a second,
or a minute, or an hour,
and you ride the late-model
euphoria till you burn up the tank.
Great way to get around,
you muse, as you add one
more sheet to the log. Yet
soon the fog descends again,
the scrim of its pearly white
dark, in its own way,
as the night. It's a faith
you hold on to, that
the attending will not cease,
that the dog bible
penned by the old Job
you have become
will continue to flow.
This is the job you
applied for and took,
paid by the page
for witnessing the weather
rolling in and away.

MOB

Look, a crowd of kindred souls
has gathered for this push-and-pull
to lift itself upon its golden
pedestal of pomp and bull.
"We're good," they roar, "you're bad!"
through hyperbolic bullish horns.
"We're right, you're wrong!"
repeats this kick-ass wound-up throng.
Sometimes one hellion is a crowd,
but worse is when a mob blends one.
With three's-a-crowd times hundreds,
nice folks transform to hellions.
This mob stomps staunchly stern.
(Amusing, seen from roofs.)
They're too smart for their good,
yet show strong primate proof:
Mad crowds exhibit all the signs
of crass chimpanzee-hood.
The mob begins to gyre,
pirouettes to hurricane:
angry clenched placards thrust —
their word-spears lust for pain.
All this tornadic raging heat,
once known for torches, tar,
feathers, nooses, grief.
Sure of history's mommy smile,
this solid legion's thick and stiff.
Whether lemmings or goddamned swine,
this suicide of fools runs off my cliff.

HUNGER IS A HUGE PROBLEM

in this world, but at our house
we know nothing of it,
and that brings what? Guilt,
humility, gratitude, good ole
middle class complacency?
At our house, even the dogs
eat well, especially log-shaped
Abigail, her wide shadow
following me or my wife
around the kitchen, cleaning
 bowls, or bird-dogging crumbs
that have somehow precipitated
to linoleum. The sore thumb
of first-world greed is a fat dog.
I love Abby. Would include her
in my prayers, if I said prayers.
Would ask forgiveness for the fat
around her belly, and mine,
would feel compassion and sadness
for the impoverished of the world
had that rerun of Jerry Seinfeld not
been on, during which I fell asleep.

ON GRATITUDE

Sometimes I wonder why I can't recall
all the instant switchblades of close calls.
I was aware disaster had whipped by
during those times. But I can't figure why
dangers that near don't stick inside my head.
Sure, close calls considered do bring dread.
Scary thoughts don't ever feel that nice.
But reflection is protection re thin ice
you just skated on. Same for the bald tire,
fat and full at a hundred miles per hour.
Or the old frayed rope that refused to break.
Or E. coli inside that rancid steak.
And the nurse who messed up, then repaired the dose.
Ditto those toxic fumes that smelled gross.
Maybe to God or to some other weird
force we should send up prayers of thanks.
Because one day the Gun whom we all here
are daughters and sons of won't be filled with blanks.

TREASURE HUNT

And once again for recreation we pray
our metal detectors over the mica-sparkled
clay of hard-packed drive-ins and ball fields
with their pop-tops, shotgun shells, and new
pennies; but soon we tire of the recent
and hit the almost holy ghost
settlement where nothing can be seen
but trees and bricks and cellar holes
and singing water in the creek.
With our headphones and our flat mikes
held toward the earth's poker face
we listen to the static
from the dead, Ouija our way
randomly across the forest floor for hours,
spelling out only *perhaps*.
We recognize just the tangibles,
small change in the watch pockets of the dead.
As always, money talks, and finally
we loosen its loud tongue.
With our spades, we startle the dirt
beneath the pines, rattle something down
deep like a chain: coins in the cracked
wool-wrapped decapitated head
of some dead child's china doll —
some copper, some silver
as a lost sky, a few green
with envy for the present —
with two fiery marbles, cat eyes,
a shred of red
velvet, and a torn inadvertent scrap
of cursive nineteenth century hand,
brittle, faint,

yet strong enough to move my lips
and call to mind the fragile lamb of Blake
with *if I die before I wake.*

COVER LETTER TO MYSELF

If the news were good they'd call.
You sent the requisite forty-eight
plus pages of your poorly xeroxed life
for approval to the Templar, yet
what are the chances,
with Martian screeners, judges
from Uranus,
and your snakebit history.

A bird requires a tree, and real
fish need a sea, yet years
you've hung these doubtful words
out dry on only air.
O self-fed vampire,
surviving on your own,
tasting blood, eating crow,
then riding down each night
these songs to lonesome dreams.
Sir, these X-rays need a home.

Dear God, dear
Nationally Recognized,
please bless with book
and lofty A. E. Neuman Prize
this sponge, this open pit, this
beggar's palm of need. This farmer
farming dust with fusty seed.

BIPOLARESQUE

My big rule is don't
pee on each other,
I tell the dogs as they
check out the pole.
It'd be my main sermon
for everyone if I
were a preacher. Then
just as quickly I scream
"Goddamn loud-
mouthed mockingbird —
where's my shotgun!"
Clearly you see
the downside of this cursed
manic-depression —
a life of making
inappropriate remarks
followed by hours
of brooding followed
by exhausting and
frenzied sex. And yet
the poems are fun:
breathtakingly mounted
and galloping out all
at once from behind
those giant boulders like
bushwhackers from heaven.

QUESTIONING THE VET'S CADUCEUS

And if this snake were real I bet
you'd kill it with a hoe. Like
the white-tail doe my daughter
accidentally crippled with her Dart
a mile from here one midnight
across from Eastwood Baptist Church.
Crying from the Magic Mart,
she phoned and woke me up,
and back into the dark we strove
to save that deer. Beside herself,
she stayed beside the frightened,
broken fragility in the ditch
while I phoned your service.
I called for her, I knew
what you would say:
Shoot it or get a cop to.
I can't believe you woke me for a deer.
The law was there when I returned.
My flashlight stared.
The spindly doe was lashed across the trunk
of the black and white, gutless.
Beside a pile of steaming entrails
Carroll stood.
There was no crying.
The law was there and that was that.

THE WHITE COAT

Going to the doctor is better
than death, but only slightly,
says the part of me given
to hyperbole, the part that
swears a toothache
is a nuclear explosion.
Going to the doctor, though,
is a big deal, the worst torture
associated with the sphygmo-
manometer that I begin to
anticipate and dread days before
the visit. It's always reminded
me of the part in "The Pit
and the Pendulum" where
the walls start closing in,
the ominous nurse smiling
through the puff puff puff
of her diabolically devilish
mechanical boa constrictor
squeezing the life from my arm.
"And this is just the beginning!"
screams my terrified little
heart, panting and scratching
and beating the walls –
but, alas, no help comes.
Till the end of your life,
none enter that jail of your heart
but the fear and the dark.

PROCRUSTES THE YARDMAN

Grass or legume,
woody or herbaceous, of
determinate or indeterminate
growth habit, it doth
not matter to the Toro —
juggernaut before which
all species, including the mouse,
tremble in the Saturday morning
breeze, the green blood scent
heavy in the air, conformity
the only rule, the law
without exception, no place
for Christopher Columbus here:
this world shall be flat
as the executioner's lip.

BIBLICAL

Death is death,
and that takes care
of that. But the living part
is the part I can't figure.
There's no mirror in death,
but it's life's mirror
I've never learned to read.
Was I bullied
or the bully?
The shaded
or the shadow?
Death's just blank,
but here is all
these hues and shades
with no credible
Sherwin-Williams chart.
Maybe I'm rain:
sometimes good,
sometimes bad.
And why do I hate you so?
Because I love you, neighbor,
as I love myself.

At Lawnwood

Once we have understood we are nothing, the object of all our
effort is to become nothing.

Simone Weil

AT LAWNWOOD

What a crowd turns up here,
supine beneath this jungle of turf,
shining from these clean stones.
Still, I'm feeling somehow they see
the same blinding blue as me
where heaven once was. All this reputed
repose should comfort, I suppose,
but looking down I'm stopped dead
by dirt. Yet I'll bet when they turn
and sneak a peek down death's abyss,
it's like when I survey the top of this pine,
then refocus higher to circling crows,
and again further up to the silver jet.
For surely there's subverted sky in death,
inverted, with deeper niches for profounder
rank; And the hooks of the dead, too,
spectrummed from shallow to deep, wishing
that something, as promised, would bite.
Surely that's what all this silent, still
waiting's about. Some type of fishing.

MURDER HOUSE

I've seen the TV ghost hunters do it:
find the infamous home or madhouse dorm
or ancient prison cell from hell, and sit
and claim tormented human souls ooze out
like spores from toxic mold to nauseate,
chill the air, and terrorize the hunters there.
But here, in spite of all I know about
this house, I'm like an ant in Lincoln's skull —
the walls are there, but all equipment's gone.
And all it sees is hard insensate bone
surrounding air and dust and muted light.
I'm ashamed to say that I almost go
to sleep. The only ghosts I feel are those
of trees split into planks, and freest earth
squeezed into walls of hard, plumb plaster board.
In here I'm pretty sure the deaths have died
and dumbly rest in peace. We're dust to dust;
our torment lies between. In peaceful gilded
autumn light these mindless dust motes mill.
They drift like tiny carefree bloodless sheep
through golden hills of inorganic air.
They gambol down then swirl back up again,
just like they did that sunny murder day.
Dust is dying's meekest circumstance.
Old loss of blood is moot to mindless trance.

THE DROWNED MAN

Man looks a lot like
the world, but with wrinkles.
They are the pain of being man,
that storm. Hardly a ripple
can be seen on real water.
But the mind can drown a man,
the mind can hold its head under
longer than you can hold your breath.
Like that man, real, that we found
at the edge of the river.
Floating, he had the look
of an insomniac finally dozing.
Long gone before he left,
he was a familiar catastrophe,
a bottle always breaking or sinking.
The river just happened to be there.
His lungs had been filling for years.

THAT NOISE

That noise?
It's just Mother
crawling down the hall to her death.
We've just about learned to live with it.
Last summer at the beach it all started.
In the morning we'd find these
strange tracks in the sand
where the hands and the knees
had started into the earth
like disoriented moles.
Immediately we knew,
Grandmother went the same way:
Crawling down halls
over roofs
under houses
along newly-poured sidewalks
leaving bony fossilized knee prints
all over town.
She managed to crawl through
three hospitals and two nursing homes
before wearing the skin off her knees
and bleeding to death.

DOPPLER EFFECT

Each week I make a list,
misplace the list, yet
my perspicacious wife
marks the big things
on the calendar in the hall:
doctor visit, bill that must be
paid, the art show at her school –
all the quick little vehicles
in my life's big race. I can
almost hear them approaching,
my red-letter days, getting
higher in pitch, building
with tension like sex,
until ZOOM – another chunk
of future's passed me by,
and I hear the come-and-gone
drop instantly several octaves.
In my mind's nostalgic eye,
like in the old cartoons,
I see the lingering cloud,
taste the bitter dust,
sense a familiar thirst,
and maybe need a drink.
Again, I see it's later than I think.

GHOST HUNTER

As if on a midnight
tour of infamous homes
I watch the silly TV
ghost hunts laden with
the fulsome tools and gauges
of pseudoscience, but all
I really see are the
flash-lit faces of fools
channeling Warhol.
Yet I know what a ghost
is; I know the terror. She
is the loved-one-shaped space
where my dear was,
her loveless absence.
That's the ice, the chill
running down my spine,
it's her vacuum in my now,
not some sheet-covered hooha
intruding on life.
Heat always flows
from hot to cold,
and plunges from your heart
into the void. Ghost
means gone.
The only presence
moving through this emptiness
is me.

BLUE YONDER

All left of Uncle Roland is his
God Is My Co-pilot license plate
still testifying on his rusting
wheel-less, blocked-up GMC.
I wonder where they flew,
barnstorming wild and low,
dragging whole clotheslines
of the living with them
into the breathless blue.

Nearly three generations
that I've known have flown.
I wonder how one disappears
from fully being here to where
just zero is. Now nothing stands
between me and disappearance
but the clouds, and even buzzards
know they're only air.

When I was 8, he shot us
like an arrow through the dizzy breeze
inside his Piper Cub. I giggled
through all his crazy dips and turns.
Back then that wild thin sky was fun.

Now its empty yawning bowl of blue's
turned gray, and all the gods
and uncles that I loved reside inside
of dreams and graves and urns.

THE ODDNESS

You too are momentary, even in your
longest human life, screams the dead
chipmunk, torn and flattened by the car's tire.
And being momentary in our long
lives of excruciating brevity
while being considerably considering
puts us between the rock and the hard place.
Even Great-grandfather with his mighty
94 years made only a scratch,
if even that, on the vast wall of time.
And all the beloved dogs no more than leaves
falling. This slowness that is so fast!
Oh, the older I get, the less it seems odd
that the *is* is a dream and the *isn't* so vast.

OUR TIRED OLD NEIGHBOR BABBLES

You whippersnappers think by the time
you get my age most folks you loved
and really yearn to see will be invisible
as history, except in old photographs.
Yet if my tenure here is worth a dime
I think I've learned that problem lies in words
that presume too much about location
and overquantify subtraction. Like
the trouble-making, lying preposition
that implies dead dears don't touch
here anymore because instead of being
with us sweetly here *on* Earth they're
in it as mere dust. Big difference, huh?
Yet now I know that difference mostly nil,
because I speak with Gwen, she *hears*, is *here* —
both different words that sound the same,
yet kiss like wind caressing rain.
When old, overthinking shifts a gear.
Then difference blends identical,
moves east toward that oneness
folks in India and Japan palaver on.
The thought of exiting stage left
(as little Billy's cartoons used to say)
has lost its fear for me: dirt
doesn't seem so dirty anymore,
feels friendly now as soil
where everything green grows,
bears fruit like Gwen's garden did.
(And does: we two still tend it!)
This ground's itself the Earth, home base,
our mother. It's where they went, yet are,
yes *are:* existent still! Gwen's planted,

grows; she thrives back home.
Over the river and through the woods,
to Mother Earth's house we go.
Lord, I haven't been home for years!
88 of them go so slow!

JERRY'S PROCESSION

All of us old, gray couples,
prim in our beige SUVs
are dressed to kill, to die
for, here attending our old
schoolmate's homegoing.
The queue to our own deaths
just shortened by one, with our
not-seen-in-forever old pal's subtraction.

The tone is formal but friendly.
Inside, the air seems almost asleep,
except that surrounding the family.
Yes, Jerry's memorial is placid,
its viscosity filling all the spaces
between pews in the Memory Hall.
There's the usual candle smell, perfume
those charged with demise puff out
over death, temporarily overpowering
the natural with the preternatural
in service to the supernatural. Well,

we still realize that all is not well,
that we too are shrinking fast, that
our remaining moments are diminishing
exponentially as we shrivel here in our dark
suits and somber funereal dresses,
ushering our old acquaintance
toward the perpetual earth. Yet
there is a grace to it all: not a soul
runs screaming off into the woods,
although perhaps we should.

COOL CATS

Dark as my mood, sweet Zorro sits
beside the road and mourns his
flattened mother, her brindle head
lopsided as a pear, broken, torn,
open for business to the decomposers'
deconstruction. We had 4 cats
and now I've watched them all
swirl down death's drain but one.
I'm tired of burying cats. I'm
tired of life's crass go then stop.
I know more dead than living.

If God would stroll into this bar
I'd ask him why with all his myriad rules
he'd start all these miracles he can't
finish. And I'm pretty sure he'd say,
"I finish! Oh, I finish, all right!"
Then I'd have to have another beer,
and another, ad infinitum: one
for each of the once-perky drops
in the bucket of the sad, sad sea,
collectively round and blue,
and salty as a tear.

ACKNOWLEDGEMENTS

Grateful acknowledgement is made to the editors of the following magazines in which these poems have appeared, some in slightly different form, or with different titles:

Agnes Scott Writers Festival Magazine: 'Bipolaresque'; *Dead Angel*: 'Dearests'; *E-Verse* Radio: "60s Love'; *New Arts* Review: 'Back Then,' 'Home,' 'That Noise'; *North of Oxford*: 'Closure'; *Plainsong*: 'The Drowned Man'; *Poems &Plays*: 'Poolroom', 'Witnessing Weather'; *Quiet Diamonds*: 'Cool Cats', 'Sublimation'; *Texas Poetry Calendar*: 'Re: The Lost Farm'; *Snake Nation Review*: 'Procrustes the Yardman'.

'Murder House' received an International Merit Award from *Atlanta Review*.

'Pluto's Despair' was anthologized in the *Southern Poetry Anthology: Georgia* from Texas Review Press.

The following poems were included in the chapbook *Physical Science*, winner of the 2003 Tennessee Poetry Chapbook Prize, from Poems & Plays: 'Back Then', 'Dearests', 'Home', 'The Drowned Man', 'That Noise', 'Questioning the Vet's Caduceus'.

The following poems were included in the chapbook *Pluto's Despair* from Kattywampus Press: 'Biblical', 'Bipolaresque', 'Cool Cat', 'Cover Letter to Myself', 'Practice', 'Pluto's Despair', 'Procrustes the Yardman', 'Roadkill Apocalypse', 'The Art of Surprise', 'Witnessing Weather'.

The following poems were included in the chapbook *Farm Alarm*, runner-up for Texas Review Press's 2018 Robert Phillips Poetry Chapbook Prize: 'Blue Yonder', 'Closure', 'Dad's Prior Commitment', 'Murder House', 'Re: The Lost Farm', 'The Last Word'.

The following poems appeared in the chapbook *Our Fatherlessness* from The Orchard Street Press: 'Little League Lesson', 'Our Fatherlessness', ''60s Love', 'The Photo'.

The following poems appeared in the full-length collection *The Least* from Iris Press: 'Closure', 'Murder House', and 'News Flash'.